MORRISSEY SHOT

MORRISSEY SHOT
LINDER STERLING

with an introduction by
Michael Bracewell

 HYPERION
New York

JUN (1) 1997
180.92
STE

First published in Great Britain in 1992 by Martin Secker &
Warburg Limited.

Edited by Robin Robertson

Designed by Chris Shamwana

**The photographer is grateful to Marshall Walker for the
printing of the photographs.**
ISBN 1-56282-773-1

First U.S. Edition

10 9 8 7 6 5 4 3 2 1

INTRODUCTION

'You're neither unnatural, nor abominable, nor mad; you're as much a part of what people call nature as anyone else; only you're unexplained as yet – you've not got your niche in creation. But some day that will come, and meanwhile don't shrink from yourself, but just face yourself calmly and bravely. Have courage; do the best you can with your burden. But above all be honourable. Cling to your honour for the sake of those others who share the same burden. For their sakes show the world that people like you and they can be quite as selfless and fine as the rest of mankind. Let your life go to prove this – it would be a really great life-work, Stephen.'
Radclyffe Hall, *The Well Of Loneliness*, 1928

And I am a living sign.
Morrissey

Throughout his career Morrissey has attracted extreme words: fanaticism, devotion, reverence, guru, genius, adoration, love. The photographs in this book reveal that these superlatives refer to something quite real. In a world which has had ample time to weary of transitory heroes, the adulation and controversy with which Morrissey is surrounded has intensified. Now, more than ever, Morrissey and his work provoke an extreme reaction. It can be argued that any phenomenon which provokes an extreme reaction is a phenomenon which transcends theory. There are thousands of learned books about art, but not one of them explains what art is. A digest of this observation can be found in Wilde's preface to *The Picture of Dorian Gray*. Indeed, one could take any of the myriad essays which have been written about Morrissey, and replace it – with impunity – with any single sentence from Wilde's prefatory essay. The rest, one feels, is simply so much cod-semiology. This, of course, annoys pop journalists. Morrissey, as these images prove, has escaped the quantifying grasp of cultural theory.

I asked one of Morrissey's fans once who his second favourite
artist was and he said he didn't have one. It's like he's a guru
or something. – Howie Klein, Vice President, Sire Records.

A Morrissey concert: the inexplicable being pursued by the insatiable. Irony and lawlessness vie for position as the presiding genius. Morrissey, clearly, is known to embody some rare source of emotion; he inspires a violent celebration. If one is tempted, cynically, to argue this point, one has only to study those photographs in this book which document the ceaseless and determined attempts by fans to demonstrate their identification with Morrissey. Whilst most large pop concerts pursue their own rituals, in the case of *Kill Uncle* there was a unique mixture of football-crowd solidarity and lone pilgrimage. Time and time again, in these photographs, one can read a story: the individual who reaches out of the crowd (at immense personal risk) to achieve a moment of intimacy.

I would follow him into any fight. – Unknown Morrissey Fan, Dublin.

He's all I've got; he's all I want. – Unknown Morrissey Fan, Hammersmith.

Morrissey has touched a particular nerve in his international audience, and thus has made articulate a desire possessed by many to make a romance out of loneliness, and to celebrate a longing for love, glamour, or even mere acceptance. His performance, on one level, embodies this process of longing. In this much, Morrissey and his fans represent a democracy: as Morrissey sings about the impossibility of intimacy, so his fans act out, by intense demonstration, their own individual, intimate relationships with him. In this way a spectacular dialogue has been established between Morrissey and his audience, the inspiration of which lies as much in an acknowledgement of shared reference points as it does in pop hysteria. The discrepancy between the riotous behaviour of Morrissey's concert audiences, and their gentle intentions, does much to define the attitude which Morrissey is seen to embody.

However one approaches a description of Morrissey, one will be met by a paradox. He is credited with inspiring a generation of apprentice poets to pirouette upon one foot in their bedrooms; at the same time, running contrary to this supposed incitement to painful sensitivity, his concerts are exuberant, even dangerous, affairs. But this is not the bovine sensibility which seeks to express itself at any tawdry 'rock spectacular'; this is a passionate gesture of support which suddenly breaks free of reason and becomes an emotional dialogue. Morrissey presents an aesthetic to his fans which demands a sense of collaboration. Where Prince or Madonna might reveal their art – behind glass as it were – Morrissey hurls his into the living-rooms of people's minds.

Linder's great achievement in this book, photographically, has been to hold her subject up to the light and consider it from many angles: the performance, the fans, the process and administration of touring, the rare moments of relaxation, the spontaneous incident and the simple image which speaks volumes about the pop idol who is impossible to define. Thus, *Morrissey Shot* is a unique document, not only with regard to the clarity and the drama of the images, but also in terms of its intimacy. Studio portraits and photo-journalism often fail to present more than one aspect of their subject; Linder's photographs, with their astute interpretation of time, place, and personality, explore moments which double as states of mind. There is a sequence of photographs, for instance, which captures the occasion when a fan embraced Morrissey during a concert as Morrissey remained immobile, with his eyes covered. Students of body language could write a doctoral thesis about such an image. A picture of Morrissey shaking hands with two polite Japanese girls becomes curiously epic: in this photograph, where the Lancastrian pop star comes face to face with oriental deference, there is such a concealed cultural struggle that one is reminded of a Victorian narrative painting which would be entitled 'Their Big Day' or 'Hands Across The Sea'. When Morrissey played in Japan, during the *Kill Uncle* tour, strictly policed fans were ordered by the venue authorities to 'check in' their bouquets – for which they were issued numbered tickets – prior to entering the stadium. There was no such restraint at other venues, where the stage swiftly became slippery with the fragrant debris of thrown flowers.

But perhaps the most telling image in this book is that of Morrissey lost in thought, studying the view from a window: his expression is off-set by his black clothes; upon his lapel there is a tiny badge of Great Britain, made out of an enamelled Union Jack. This is Morrissey as the solitary ambassador: a lonely, isolated figure, who carries so much invisible emotional luggage.

Theorists could argue that Morrissey is the direct inheritor of a line of English wit which connects him to Firbank and Alan Bennett by way of the poems of Sir John Betjeman and British cinema of the 1960s. And yet this is only part of the equation. In order to understand Morrissey's intense appeal, and the violent celebration which attends him, one must review his writing whilst realising the power of his singing. Morrissey has a voice which can soar, dispelling any notion of feyness by presenting the persona of a rock'n'roll crooner. He is therefore the only singer who can combine the glamour of the young Elvis Presley with a lyrical style which merges confessional poetry with the language of Gilbert & Sullivan. Perversely, the world of pop music is largely intolerant of intelligent – let alone 'intellectual' – rebels. At root, most pop music and its audience is deeply conservative. By working alone, indurate to fads or fashionability, Morrissey has both maintained and developed a defiantly unique stance.

The *Kill Uncle* tour was an event which surpassed even American standards of pop hysteria. Towards its conclusion it had become dangerous to continue.

It's as though he was burning too brightly. – Member of tour personnel.

As Linder's photographs enable one to witness the extraordinary ambience of *Kill Uncle*, the following statistics tell their own remarkable story: New York's Madison Square Garden (seating more than 20,000) sold out in a morning; tickets for the concert at the LA Forum were all sold in 14 minutes – a thousand per minute; the 18,000-seat Pacific Amphitheater in San Diego was sold out in an hour. In terms of merchandising, the *Kill Uncle* tour broke the record previously held by U2. This book should be studied with an eye to these facts.

I once asked Morrissey whether he felt the relationship which he had with his fans was that of being actually loved (as one might love one's wife or husband) by millions of strangers. He replied: 'I wish somebody else could answer this; I would like to think that I'm considered to be a real person, singing for a real need – it's actually that simple.'

Can such a concept be simple? *Morrissey Shot*, as photographic art, explores this fascinating question.

My presence, like a robe pontifical,
Ne'er seen but wonder'd at.
Henry The Fourth, Part One.

Michael Bracewell

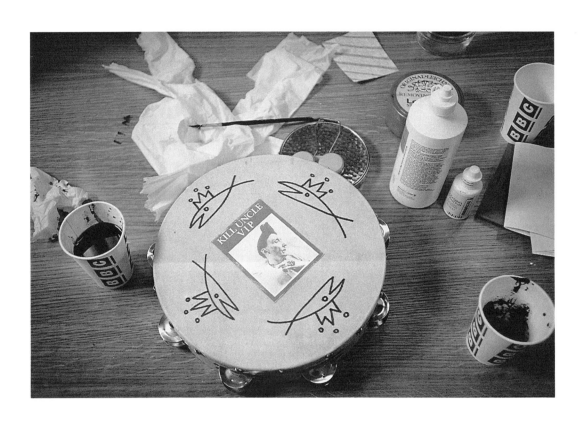

Caird Hall, Dundee   15/5/91

Empire Theatre, Liverpool 24/7/91

Capitol Theatre, Aberdeen 14/5/91
8

Caird Hall, Dundee 15/5/91

Alain Whyte – guitars

Boz Boorer – guitars

Gary Day – the bass

Spencer Cobrin – the drums

The National, Kilburn, London   3/10/91

The Sun Palace, Fukuoka, Japan   27/8/91

Madison Square Garden, New York 13/7/91

Nassau Coliseum, New York   11/11/91

Caird Hall, Dundee 15/5/91

Madison Square Garden, New York   13/7/91

De Montfort Hall, Leicester   8/10/91

Nassau Coliseum, New York 11/11/91

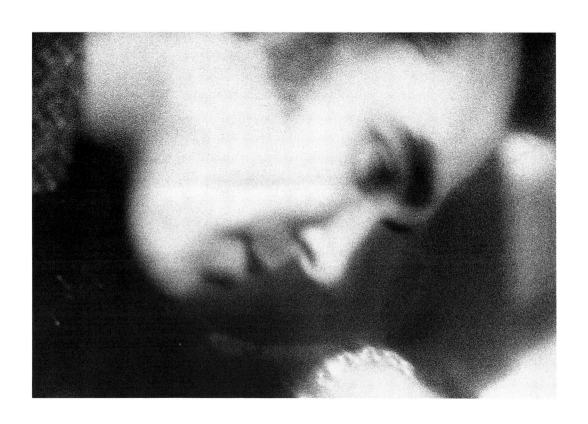

Wembley Arena, London   20/7/91

Bullet train Hikari #13 between Osaka and Fukuoka   26/8/91

Bethnal Green, East London   5/10/91

King Georges Hall, Blackburn   26/7/91
33

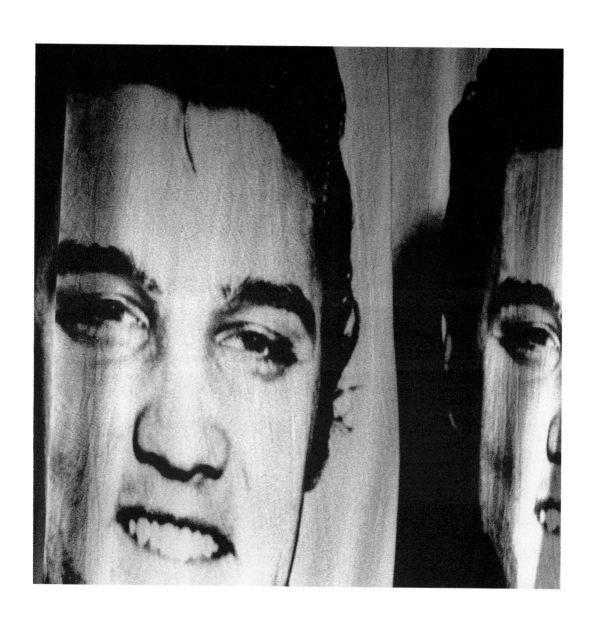

Aragon Ballroom, Chicago   8/11/91

The Sports Arena, San Diego   30/5/91

California 31/5/91
38

King Georges Hall, Blackburn   26/7/91

Aragon Ballroom, Chicago   8/11/91

Nassau Coliseum, New York 11/11/91

Wembley Arena, London   20/7/91

The Forum, Los Angeles   2/6/91

Wapping, London   21/2/92

East End, London   5/10/91

Sunset Boulevard 4/6/91

La Cienega Boulevard 3/6/91

Budokan, Tokyo 2/9/91

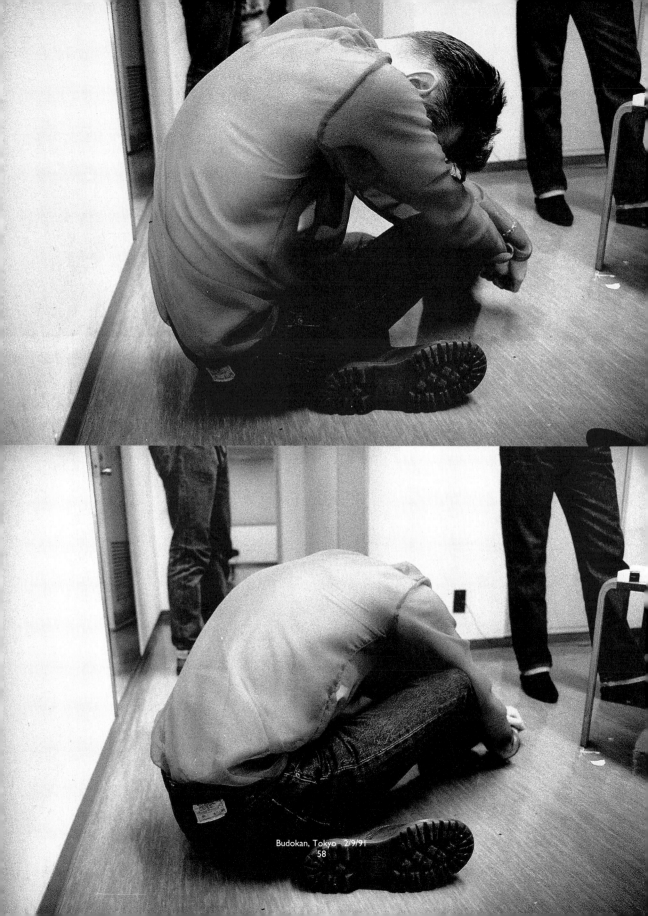

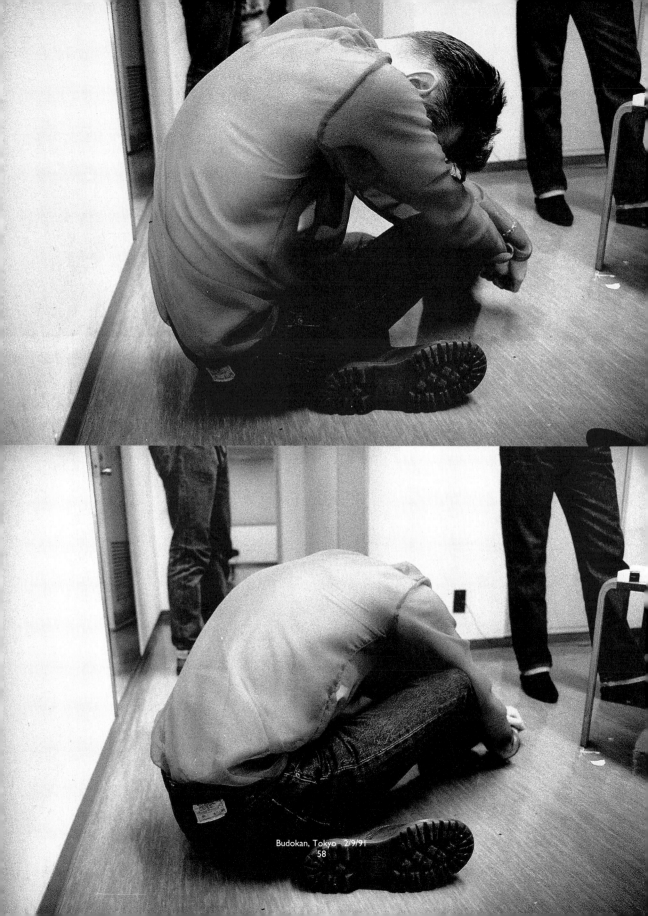

Budokan, Tokyo 2/9/91
58

Aragon Ballroom, Chicago   8/11/91

The Point, Dublin   29/9/91
62

Jones Beach Amphitheater, Long Island   10/7/91

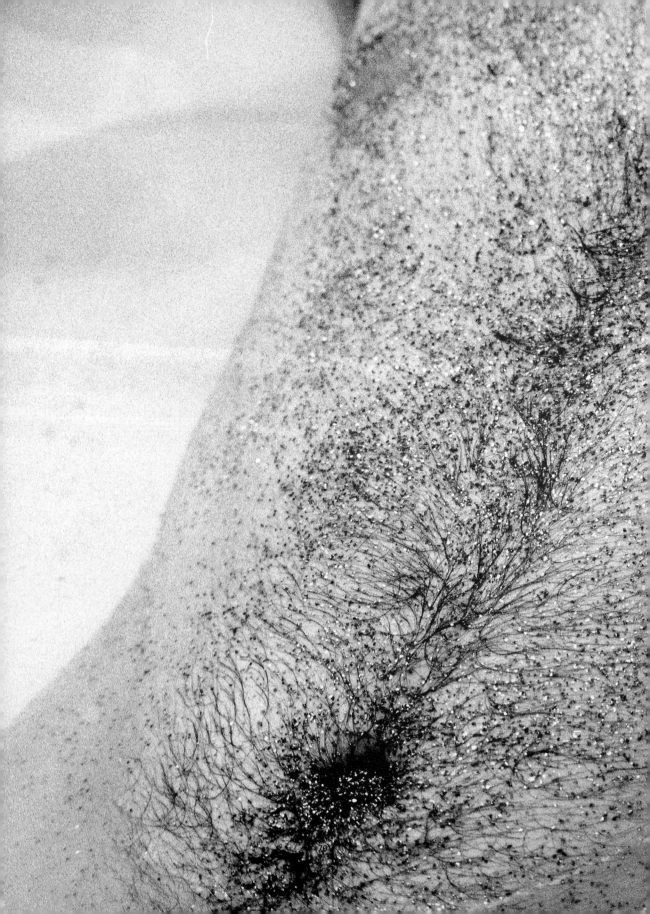

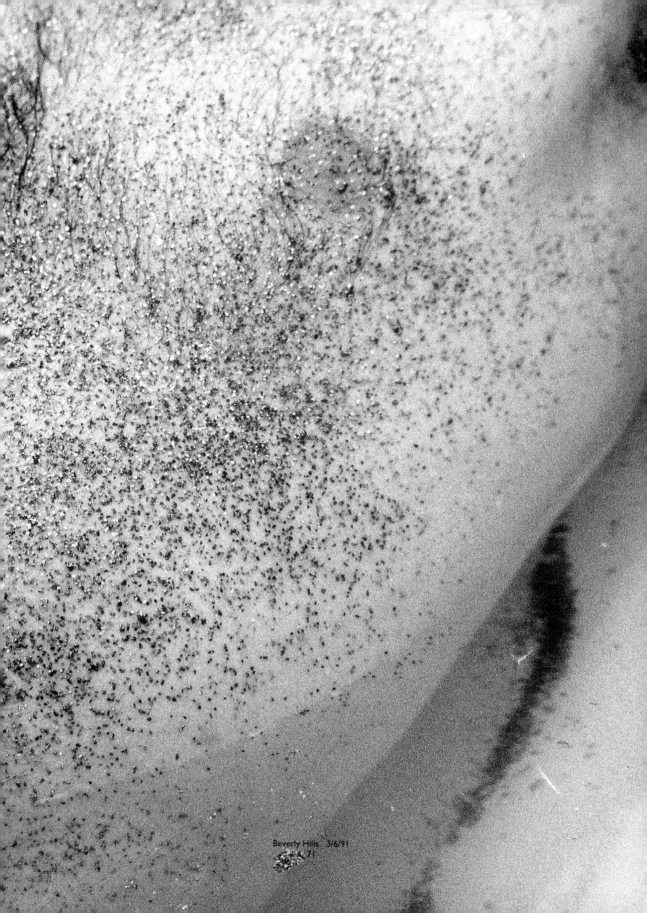

Beverly Hills 3/6/91
71

David Bowie, Los Angeles 2/6/91   Sinead O'Connor, Cheshire 18/7/91

Sparks, Westwood 1/6/91   Michael Stipe and Rickie Lee Jones, New York City   13/7/91

Hollywood 4/6/91

San Diego   30/5/91

Capitol Studios, Hollywood   3/6/91

Caird Hall, Dundee   15/5/91

The Sports Arena, San Diego   30/5/91

Osaka, Japan   25/8/91

The Sun Palace, Fukuoka, Japan   27/8/91

San Diego   30/5/91

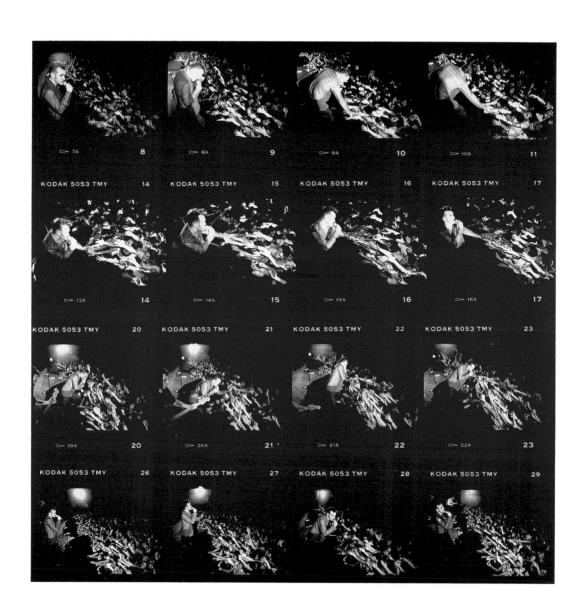

The Sun Palace, Fukuoka, Japan   27/8/91

Tokyo   30/8/91

Hammersmith Odeon, London 4/10/91

MORRISSEY

Tシャツ (X・XL) ￥3,500
ポスター (小) ￥1,000
ポスター (大) ￥1,500
￥1,000

The Sun Palace, Fukuoka, Japan 27/8/91

94

The Forum, Los Angeles 2/6/91
91

The County Bowl, Santa Barbara   7/6/91
92

Manhattan 12/7/91
93

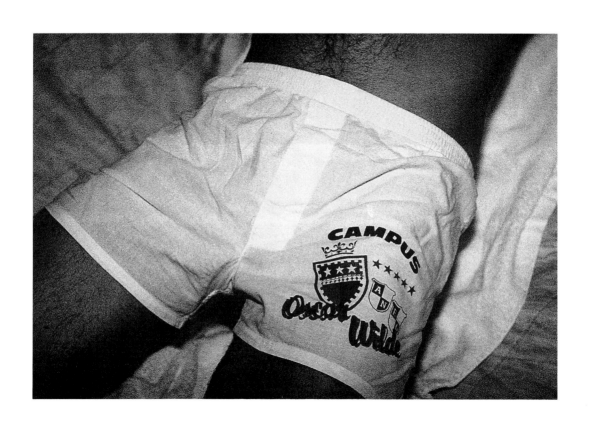

The Sports Arena, San Diego   30/5/91

California Expo, Sacramento   9/6/91

Hammersmith Odeon, London 4/10/91

Glasgow 28/7/91
100

King Georges Hall, Blackburn   26/7/91
101

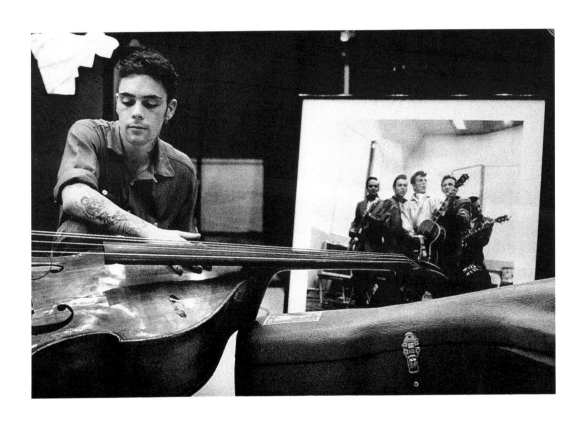

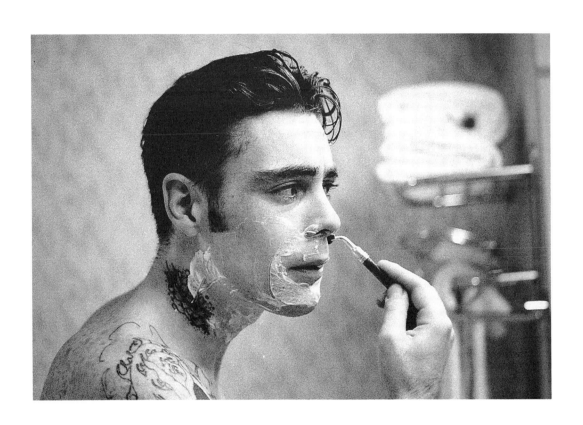

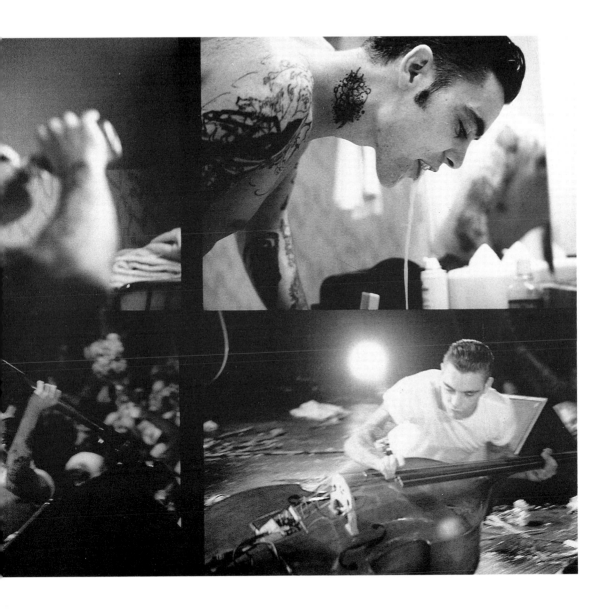

Madison Square Garden, New York   13/7/91

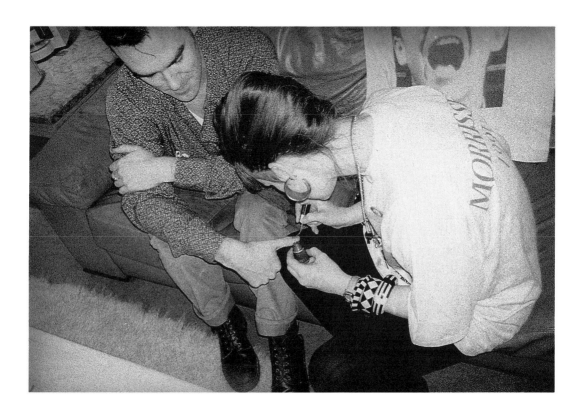

Madison Square Garden, New York   13/7/91

Wembley Arena   20/7/91

De Montfort Hall, Leicester   8/10/91

Pacific Amphitheater, Orange County, Los Angeles   1/6/91

The Sports Arena, San Diego   30/5/91

The Sports Arena, San Diego   30/5/91

Madison Square Garden, New York   13/7/91

Royal Concert Hall, Glasgow   28/7/91

The County Bowl, Santa Barbara   7/6/91

The Sports Arena, San Diego   30/5/91
131

Capitol Theatre, Aberdeen   14/5/91

Brixton Academy, London   21/7/91

The Forum, Los Angeles   2/6/91

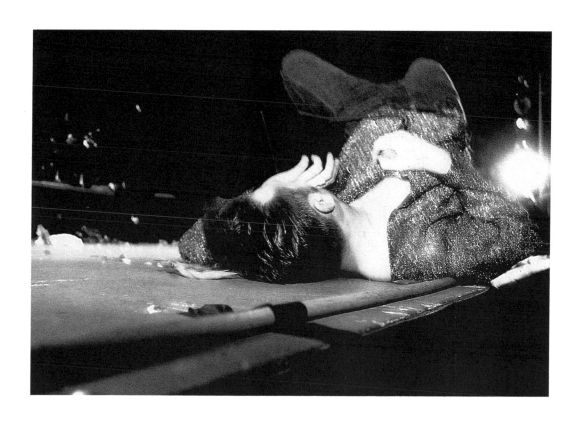

The Sports Arena, San Diego   30/5/91

780.92   paper
Ste

Sterling, Linder

Morrissey shot

DATE DUE CL (1) ✔
